GROWING GARDENS

Fruit Gardens

BY ANGELA LIM

Kids Core

An Imprint of Abdo Publishing

abdobooks.com

abdobooks.com

Published by Abdo Publishing, a division of ABDO, PO Box 398166, Minneapolis, Minnesota 55439.

Printed in the United States of America, North Mankato, Minnesota.
052025
092025

THIS BOOK CONTAINS
RECYCLED MATERIALS

Cover Photo: Shutterstock Images
Interior Photos: Tatevosian Yana/Shutterstock Images, 4–5; Anna Frank/E+/Getty Images, 6; Monkey Business Images/Shutterstock Images, 8; Shutterstock Images, 10–11, 14, 25, 28 (top), 28 (bottom), 29 (top), 29 (bottom); Amallia Eka/Shutterstock Images, 12; Artem Oleshko/Shutterstock Images, 16–17; Dmytro Zinkevych/Shutterstock Images, 18; SDI Productions/E+/Getty Images, 19; Goodboy Picture Company/E+/Getty Images, 21; iStockphoto, 22, 26; Renata Angerami/E+/Getty Images, 24

Editor: Christa Kelly
Series Designer: Katharine Hale

Library of Congress Control Number: 2024948990

Publisher's Cataloging-in-Publication Data

Names: Lim, Angela, author.
Title: Fruit gardens / by Angela Lim
Description: Minneapolis, Minnesota: Abdo Publishing, 2026 | Series: Growing gardens | Includes online resources and index.
Identifiers: ISBN 9781098297398 (lib. bdg.) | ISBN 9798384919919 (ebook)
Subjects: LCSH: Gardens--Juvenile literature. | Gardening--Juvenile literature. | Fruit--Juvenile literature. | Horticulture--Juvenile literature.
Classification: DDC 634--dc23

CONTENTS

Strawberries can be eaten raw, blended into drinks, or baked into pastries.

CHAPTER 1

A Sweet Summer Treat

Maggie swung a bucket in her hand. She and her dad headed to the backyard. They had planted strawberries together in the spring. Now it was summer. She hoped the strawberries would finally be ready to harvest.

Strawberry seedlings take two to three months to make fruit.

It was Maggie's first time gardening. She and her dad checked the plants often. They pulled up weeds that sprouted near the strawberries. They watered the plants when the soil was dry.

Maggie loved watching the plants grow. New leaves sprouted. Bees buzzed around the plants' white blossoms. The petals began to drop away. Then strawberries appeared. At first, they were small and green. But over the summer, they swelled and turned red. Now they were ready to harvest! Maggie carefully plucked a strawberry and took a big bite. It was the best strawberry she had ever eaten!

Joys of Gardening

Gardening is a great way to spend time outdoors. Spending time in nature can reduce stress. It can improve mental health.

Fruit or Vegetable?

Many people think of tomatoes and cucumbers as vegetables. But scientifically, these plants are fruits! A fruit is the part of a plant that holds seeds. The word *vegetable* is a cooking term. This term describes plant parts, including some fruits, that are not sweet.

Gardening teaches people about plants.

Starting a fruit garden can help physical health too. People use many muscles when gardening. Fruit gardens can also improve a person's diet. Fruits have **vitamins** that keep the body healthy.

Fruit gardening takes time. Gardeners must plan and care for their gardens. But the rewards are sweet and tasty!

Primary Source

Fruits tend to have a lot of natural sugar. Some people think this makes fruits unhealthy. But **nutritionist** Lisa Valente disagrees. She says:

> The benefits to eating fruit definitely outweigh any downsides. Fruit has so many great nutritional qualities and it just happens to taste good.

Source: Lauren Wicks. "Here's Why You Should Eat Fruit Even Though It Contains Sugar." *Eating Well*, 27 June 2024, eatingwell.com. Accessed 13 Sept. 2024.

Point of View

What is the author's point of view? What is your point of view? Write a short essay about how they are similar and different.

There are more than 2,000 species of fruits.

CHAPTER 2

Planning a Fruit Garden

Every plant has different needs. These needs are important to keep in mind when planning a fruit garden. Space is one need. Some fruits grow on trees. Trees need a lot of room to grow. Other fruits grow on bushes.

Blueberries can grow in pots. People can grow them on porches.

Still others grow on vines. These fruits can be good options for smaller gardens.

An area's **climate** also affects the type of fruit a gardener can grow. Some fruits need warm temperatures year-round. Others can survive in cold conditions. However, they typically do not produce fruit in the winter.

Sunlight is another need. Most fruit plants need six to eight hours of direct sunlight each day. But some berries grow best in partial sunlight.

The amount of water a fruit plant needs also varies. Many berries require **moist** soil to grow. They need to be watered frequently. Newly planted fruit trees need a lot of water. **Established** fruit trees need less water.

Growing Vines

Some fruits, such as grapes, grow on vines. These fruits can work well in small gardens. People can grow vine plants near a wooden frame called a trellis. The trellis helps the plant grow upward rather than along the ground. This uses less garden space.

What Do Fruit Plants Need?

Fruit	Space Needed	Amount of Sunlight	Amount of Water	Ideal Climate
Blueberry	2 to 2.5 feet (0.6–0.8 m)	More than 6 hours of sunlight each day	1 inch (2.5 cm) per week during growing season; 4 inches (10 cm) per week while fruit is ripening	Humid, northern climates with chilly winters and cool summers
Grape	6 feet (2 m)	More than 6 hours of sunlight each day	0.5 to 1 inch (1.3–2.5 cm) per week	Depends on variety, but does best in humid climates with warm summers and cool winters
Apple	10 to 25 feet (3–8 m)	At least 8 hours of sunlight a day	Newly planted trees need 5 gallons (19 L) one to three times a week; established trees need about 1 inch (2.5 cm) per week	Depends on variety, but does best in humid climates with warm summers and cool winters

Each fruit plant has different growing needs.

Growing Time

When deciding which fruits to plant, gardeners should consider how long each plant takes to grow. Fruit trees take several years to start growing fruit. But then they produce fruit for many years. Blueberry plants follow this pattern too.

Other plants produce fruit after only a few months. But they produce less fruit every year. The plants must be replaced after a few years. Strawberries are an example of these types of fruits.

Further Evidence

Look at the website below. Does it give any new evidence to support Chapter Two?

Blueberries Growing Guide

abdocorelibrary.com/fruit-gardens

While preparing a garden space, gardeners should break up the soil. This allows water and air to get to plants' roots.

CHAPTER 3

Growing Fruit

Once gardeners have planned their gardens, they can prepare a space for their plants. Small plants, such as strawberries, need empty places to grow. Gardeners should remove any weeds. These plants compete with garden plants for **nutrients**.

Newly planted fruit trees should be watered about three times each week.

Fruit trees do not need empty places to grow. But they still need to have their soil prepared. The soil the tree will be planted in should be broken up with a shovel. This will give space for the tree's roots to grow.

People can buy seedlings from garden stores.

Planting Fruit

The garden is finally ready to be planted! Gardeners can decide whether to grow their plants from seeds or seedlings. Some fruits can be grown either way. But fruit trees usually have to be bought as seedlings. This is because fruit trees grown from seeds tend to produce fruit that tastes bad.

When planting, gardeners should pay careful attention to any instructions on seed packets or seedling containers. These instructions usually tell gardeners how deep to plant the seeds or seedlings. They also tell gardeners how far apart each plant should be. Following these instructions gives the plants enough depth and space to properly grow.

Garden Care

Fruit plants need to be watered regularly. Gardeners should water close to the roots. Soil should be kept moist but not flooded.

Plants also need to be frequently weeded. Weeds can harm the growth of new plants. Gardeners can remove weeds by hand.

Weeds should be removed before they make seeds and reproduce.

They can also use chemicals. But these chemicals can be harmful to people and animals. They can also harm plants.

Straw mulch can protect strawberry plants from dying during the winter.

Mulch can help prevent weeds. Mulch is a protective layer of material. Many materials can be used as mulch. Many people use wood chips or straw. In addition to preventing weeds, mulch also helps keep soil moist.

Many gardeners have to deal with pests. Animals such as deer and rabbits often try to eat the plants. Netting and fences can help prevent these animals from damaging a garden. Bugs can damage plants too. Pesticides can help. Pesticides are chemicals that kill bugs. However, many pesticides are harmful to people and the environment.

Fertilizing plants is another part of garden care. Fertilizers provide plants with nutrients. They help plants grow and produce fruit.

Natural Pesticides

Gardeners can use natural pesticides to get rid of insects. Garlic spray is a mixture of crushed garlic and water. It can help **repel** insects. A spray of vegetable oil mixed with soap can also be used as a pesticide.

Food scraps eventually break down into compost. This can be used as a natural fertilizer.

Spring is the best time to fertilize plants. Gardeners can add fertilizer to the soil around established plants.

Picking fruits a little early can prevent them from being eaten by pests.

Harvest Time

Harvest time is an exciting part of gardening. Some gardens can produce fruit year-round. But this depends on the climate.

Gardeners can learn to tell when fruits are ready to be harvested. Fruits tend to soften as they become ripe. Peaches and apricots are ready to be picked when they start to soften. They can then continue to ripen off the tree.

Cantaloupes are ready to harvest about 80 to 90 days after planting.

Many fruits change color. For example, unripe strawberries are green. Ripe strawberries are bright red. Other fruits, such as cantaloupes, smell sweet when they are ready to be harvested.

Fruits should be harvested with care. A gentle twisting motion is all it takes to loosen ripe apples and pears from a tree. Berries are delicate. Gardeners should grab berries gently.

Growing a fruit garden takes careful planning and hard work. But it can be very rewarding. Gardening is a fun hobby with tasty results!

Explore Online

Visit the website below. Does it give any new information about caring for a fruit garden that wasn't in Chapter Three?

How to Start a Fruit Garden

abdocorelibrary.com/fruit-gardens

Garden Plants

Strawberry

Strawberries grow on low-growing plants. Their fruit can be harvested about two to three months after planting.

Peach

Peaches grow on trees. Peach trees begin to produce fruit after about three years.

Fig

Figs grow on trees. Most varieties take about three years to start producing fruit.

Kiwis grow on vines. It takes about three to four years for a kiwi plant to first produce fruit.

Kiwi

Glossary

climate
the long-term weather pattern of a certain area; also, an area with a specific long-term weather pattern

established
having a well-developed root system

moist
damp

nutrients
substances that living things need to grow and stay healthy

nutritionist
a person who studies how food impacts human health

repel
to make something stay away

vitamins
chemicals that help the body grow and develop

Online Resources

To learn more about growing fruit gardens, visit our free resource websites below.

Visit **abdocorelibrary.com** or scan this QR code for free Common Core resources for teachers and students, including vetted activities, multimedia, and booklinks, for deeper subject comprehension.

Visit **abdobooklinks.com** or scan this QR code for free additional online weblinks for further learning. These links are routinely monitored and updated to provide the most current information available.

Learn More

Gadzekpo, Darryl, and Ella Phillips. *From Plant to Plate.* DK, 2024.

Hämeenaho-Fox, Satu. *My First Garden.* DK, 2023.

Lilley, Matt. *Vegetable Gardens.* Abdo, 2026.

Index

About the Author

Angela Lim is an MFA student in poetry at Indiana University. She enjoys reading in the park.